EMBELLISHED COOKIES

EMBELLISHED COOKIES

Sweet and Stylish Treats For All Occasions

ROBYN KING

First published in 2016 by New Holland Publishers Pty Ltd
London • Sydney • Auckland

The Chandlery Unit 704 50 Westminster Bridge Road London SE1 7QY United Kingdom
1/66 Gibbes Street Chatswood NSW 2067 Australia
5/39 Woodside Ave Northcote, Auckland 0627 New Zealand

www.newhollandpublishers.com

A record of this book is held at the British Library and the National Library of Australia.

ISBN 9781742577395

Managing Director: Fiona Schultz
Publisher: Diane Ward
Project Editor: Holly Willsher
Designer: Lorena Susak and Peter Guo
Production Director: Olga Dementiev

Printer: Toppan Leefung Printing Limited

10 9 8 7 6 5 4 3 2 1

Keep up with New Holland Publishers on Facebook
www.facebook.com/NewHollandPublishers

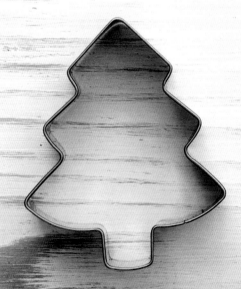

Contents

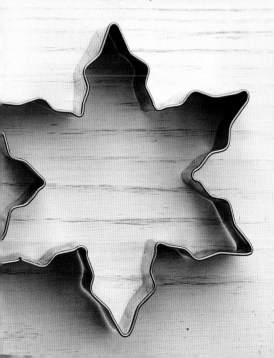
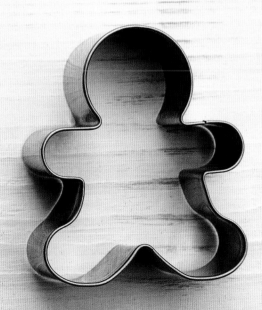

INTRODUCTION

Making beautiful cookies for family and friends is not only fun but very rewarding.

Inspiration for making such treats comes from the smiling faces and the excitement when gorgeous cookies are given as a gift or presented on a table for celebrations. I especially love to present these special treats as bouquets which make beautiful gifts for all occasions.

Not all cookie recipes are suitable for decorating when using the methods shown in this book, so I have included three of my favorites which have proven to be very popular. The recipes are very versatile and can be changed to have different flavors, nuts and spices added to the mixture to give your own individual touch to your cookies.

When baking cookies for the bouquets, wooden skewers can be inserted into the cookie dough before they go into the oven. This allows the cookies to be presented upright in the bouquet or they can be individually wrapped with a bow or a decorative tie. Remember, presentation is just as important as the product itself.

I truly enjoy sharing my knowledge of many years with others and hope that you find inspirational ideas and tips throughout this book to help you get started.

Enjoy!

ESSENTIAL
EQUIPMENT

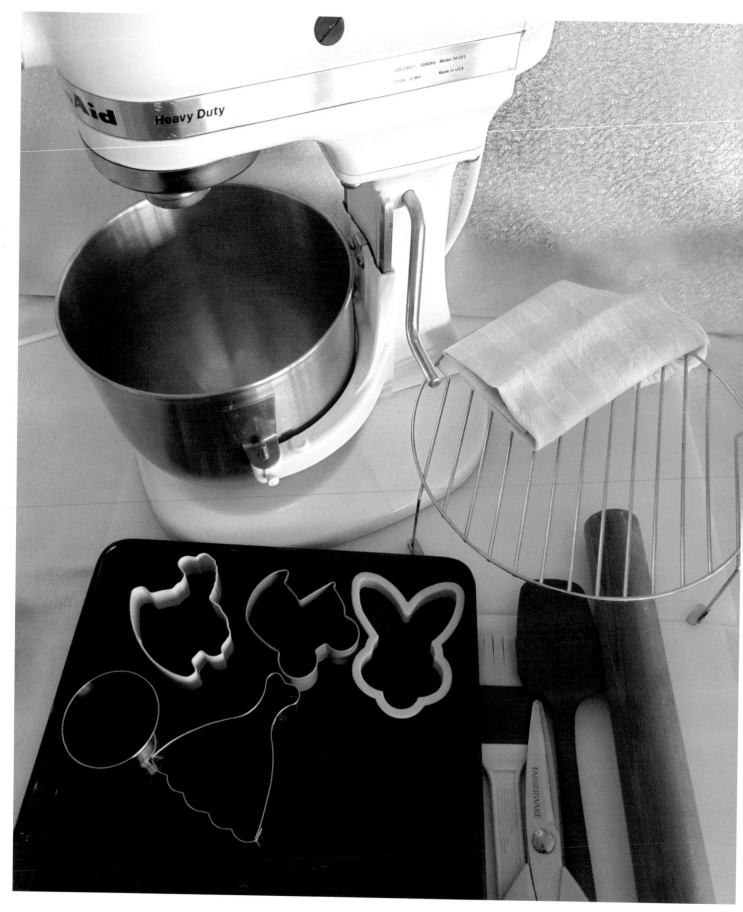

Baking Equipment

Anyone can make a cookie like a professional. There is not a lot of equipment needed in order to create a beautiful cookie. The important thing is to have a good recipe and some simple cutters which give a clean and well defined edge.

A large rolling pin is also helpful as it is easier to roll the cookie dough evenly. I like to line the baking tray with baking paper to ensure that the cookies don't stick, it also stops the base from browning faster than the top.

- Mixer
- Cooling wire
- Rolling pin
- Tea towel
- Spatula
- Cookie cutters
- Baking tray
- Baking paper

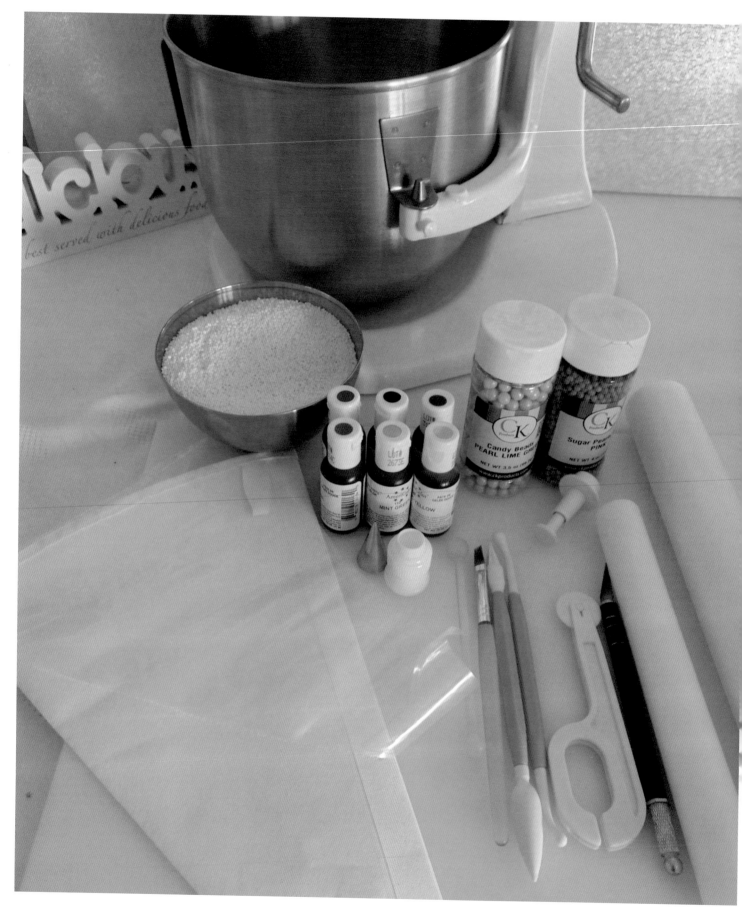

Decorating Products

The choices for decorating products are endless, there is so much available in both supermarkets and specialty cake stores.

I have listed some of the most commonly used items.

- Food coloring
- Sprinkles
- Cachous (*small metallic balls which are edible*)
- Paintbrush
- Balling tool
- Cutting blade
- Rose spirit (*this can be used to mix with your luster powders to create your own luster paint. Rose spirit also allows food color to dry quickly without ruining your sugar decoration*)
- Tylose powder (*also called CMC is a hardening agent, it is added to fondant to make it firmer which makes the fondant easier to remove from a mold, it also helps the fondant to set and hold shape*)
- Greaseproof paper
- Piping tips and couplers

BASIC RECIPES

Shortbread Biscuits

Shortbread is a versatile mix to use for cookie decorating. It bakes beautifully, keeping its shape well. This recipe works well when other flavors or spices are added. I have noted a few suggestions below the recipe.

PREPARATION: 15 MINUTES

COOKING: 25 MINUTES

Ingredients

500 g (17½ oz) unsalted butter

250 g (9 oz) superfine sugar (caster sugar)

1 teaspoon vanilla essence

125 g (4½ oz) rice flour

650 g (23 oz) all-purpose (plain flour)

1 teaspoon cinnamon or mixed spice (optional)

Method

1. Preheat oven to low 175°C (347°F).
2. Beat the butter, sugar and vanilla together until light and fluffy.
3. Sift together the flours and spices.
4. Add the combined flour and spices to the butter mixture and mix together until combined.
5. Roll out the pastry to just under 1 cm (½ in) thickness and cut out shapes using the desired cutters.
6. Place onto a greased baking tray.
7. Bake for 30 minutes or until a pale golden color and then leave to cool.

Note* The Shortbread recipe is especially tasty when 1 teaspoon of cinnamon is added to the flour.

This recipe could also be made as a chocolate flavored shortbread by simply adding 55 g (2 oz) of cocoa powder, however leave 75 g (3 oz) flour out of the mix as it will be too dry.

If your desire is to add nuts or chocolate chips, be sure to chop them very small so as to avoid the mixture from becoming lumpy on the surface. To decorate successfully, attention needs to be given to the evenness of the cookie surface.

Gingerbread

The smell of gingerbread baking in the oven is to die for. The aromatic spices in this recipe is just the right balance, not too gingery but very tasty. When baking gingerbread, the baking time is of high importance as leaving them in the oven for too long will result in a bitter hard cookie.

I like mine to be lighter in color and not so hard. Every oven is different, the temperatures can vary quite a bit so use the baking time as a guide only.

PREPARATION: 20 MINUTES

COOKING: 25–35 MINUTES

Ingredients

125 g (4½ oz) brown sugar
¼ teaspoon salt
300 g (10½ oz) treacle or
    golden syrup
2 tablespoons ground ginger
½ tablespoon mixed spice
1 teaspoon cinnamon
180 g (6 oz) butter
500 g (17½ oz) all-purpose
    (plain flour)
½ teaspoon baking soda
    (bicarbonate of soda)
extra flour for rolling

Method

1. Preheat oven to 160°C (320°F) for 15 minutes.
2. In a large bowl, beat the sugar, salt, treacle or golden syrup, ginger, spices and butter with an electric mixer on medium speed for 2 minutes.
3. Add remaining ingredients and mix until mixture forms a thick dough.
4. Place on a floured work surface.
5. Roll out and cut into desired shapes.
6. Place on a baking tray lined with baking paper and bake in the oven for 25–30 minutes or until firm to touch (dough will harden as it cools).

Sugar Cookies

Sugar style cookies make a great base for your decorated masterpiece. The advantage to using this recipe is that they bake quite quickly and are less buttery than shortbread which make them the perfect choice for children's parties.

PREPARATION: 15 MINUTES

COOKING: 10 MINUTES

Ingredients
175 g (4½ oz) unsalted butter
290 g (10½ oz) superfine sugar
   (caster sugar)
1 egg and 1 egg yolk
1 teaspoon vanilla essence
1 teaspoon grated lemon rind
¼ teaspoon salt
290 g (10½ oz) all-purpose
   (plain flour)

Method
1. Preheat oven to 180°C (350°F).
2. Cream together the butter and sugar until light and fluffy, add the egg, vanilla, lemon rind and salt.
3. Add the flour and mix until combined (don't overbeat at this point as the biscuits will become tough).
4. On a floured surface bring the dough together to form a ball. Refrigerate for 30 minutes to let rest and then the dough can be rolled.
5. Roll dough to about 3 mm (⅛ in) thickness, cut out shapes with cookie cutters and place on a baking tray lined with baking paper.
6. Bake for about 10 minutes until lightly golden.

Royal Icing

This quantity makes approximately 700 g (25 oz) of Royal Icing. The recipe could be halved if only a small amount is needed.

Ingredients

3 egg whites (*egg white powder or meringue powder can be substituted for fresh egg whites) reconstitute as per manufacturers instructions to make up 120 ml (4 fl oz) then continue with recipe*

600 g (21 oz) confectioners' sugar (icing sugar), sifted (Not all may be used)

1 teaspoon lemon juice or (4 drops acetic acid)

Method

1. Place egg whites in a large bowl and mix on the slowest speed for 1 minute.
2. Add some of the sifted confectioners' sugar to the mixture and continue mixing on slow.
3. Keep adding confectioners' sugar a little at a time. When half the sugar is mixed through add the lemon juice or acid.
4. Slowly add more confectioners' sugar.
5. When the mixture looks like thick whipped cream and stands to soft peaks, it is ready to be used for piping.
6. Place in an airtight container as this icing tends to dry out very quickly.
7. If using egg whites it can be kept in the fridge for a week (bring back to room temperature before use) if using the meringue powder the mixture will last for 2–3 weeks.

Making a Piping Bag

When piping royal icing I like to use piping bags made from greaseproof paper. However plastic disposable bags work just as well.

To roll a piping bag using greaseproof paper follow the below instructions.

- Cut a square from a roll of greaseproof paper then cut again on the diagonal to give two triangular pieces.
- Hold the two pieces together to give double strength bags. Roll around your hand to form a point half way down the angled side of the paper.
- Keeping tension on the paper continue to roll around the hand keeping the point in tact, then fold at the top to secure.

Sugar Syrup

Sugar Syrup is used when sticking fondant cut outs to the baked cookie or fondant to fondant when adding the embellishments to the surface of the iced cookie.

Method
1. Sugar syrup is made from equal amounts of sugar and water
2. To make a simple syrup place 100 g (3½ oz) sugar and 100 ml (3½ fl oz) of water in a saucepan.
3. Bring to the boil, and simmer for a few minutes.
4. Once cool pour into an airtight container, this can be kept in the fridge for up to a week.
5. Use sparingly to brush onto each cookie to make the fondant stick. Alternatively, a bought piping gel can be used.

ICING TECHNIQUES AND PROJECTS

Fondant Iced Cookies

How to Use Fondant

Ready made fondant icing is available in all good supermarkets or specialty stores. Fondant can also be made at home however I find the bought ones keep for a longer period of time without going too hard and is a reliable consistency all of the time.

Decorating cookies using fondant can be made easy and simple or time can be taken to achieve creative and detailed pieces of art. Whatever design you choose to do, whether it be simple or more complex, the principal is still the same.

Using your favorite recipe, make the cookies and cut into the shape of your choice, bake and cool. Follow the instructions below and create your wonderful fondant cookies.

1. Start by coloring the fondant with the desired food coloring, then roll the fondant to a 1 mm (³⁄₆₄ in) thickness.
2. Cut out the shape using the same cutter which was used to cut out the cookie.
3. Using piping gel or sugar syrup dampen the cookie and place the fondant on top (this is the foundation for your masterpiece so cut edges cleanly, smoothing the top well in preparation for the finer details.
4. Have all the colors which are needed for the design pre colored and ready at hand, then roll out and cut out the details (for example: – use small circle cutters for wheels or roll small balls of fondant and press on for eyes).
5. Use piping gel or syrup to stick on the embellishments.

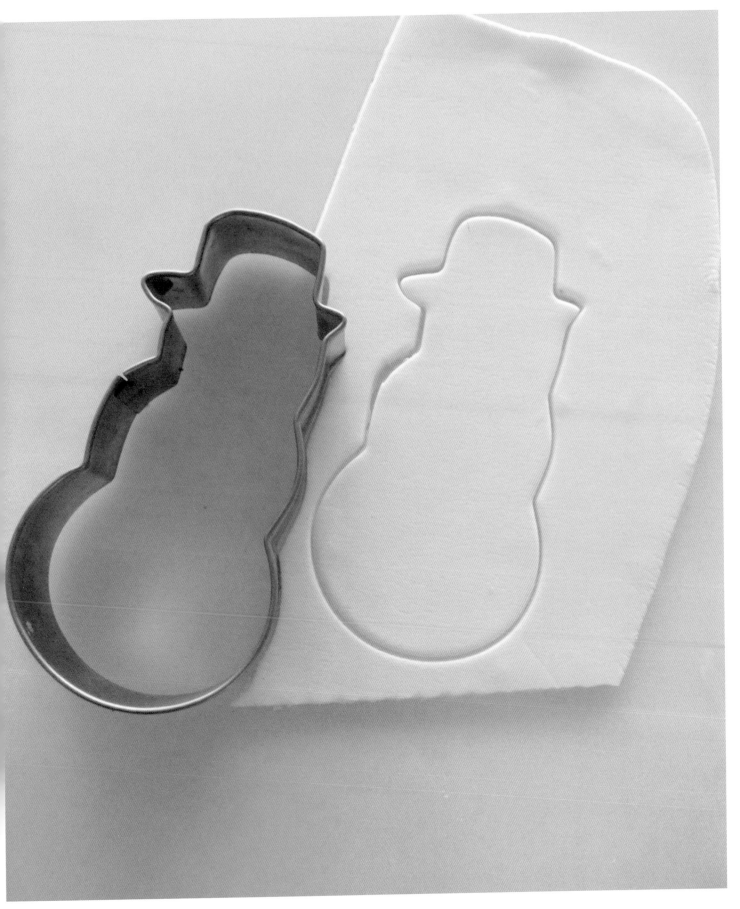

Easter Bunny Face Cookies

The perfect little treats for your Spring or Easter party. You know what they say about bunnies, and it's true! These sweet little Easter bunny cookies breed good cheer and a bushel of it!

Instructions

1. Prepare your favorite cookie dough as per cookie instructions and set aside to cool.
2. Using piping gel or sugar syrup dampen the cookie and cover with the cut out white fondant.
3. Once the cookies are covered with fondant roll some white fondant balls for the eyes and add a black fondant ball for the pupil.
4. Make teeth by cutting two oblong shapes, stick the teeth just under the nose which is made from two white balls pushed onto the nose area with a smaller pink ball just above. With a toothpick, poke some holes in where the whiskers go. Paint some eyelashes and eyebrows with a liner brush and black coloring.

Heart Cookies

Hearts for both Mother's Day or Valentine's Day are a popular choice.

Instructions

1. Prepare your favorite cookie dough as per cookie instructions and set aside to cool.
2. Using piping gel or sugar syrup dampen the cookie and cover with the cut out red fondant.
3. Roll out some extra fondant and cut out several smaller hearts in contrasting colors and stick on top with some piping gel.
4. Further enhance your design by piping tiny dots or lines around the fondant.

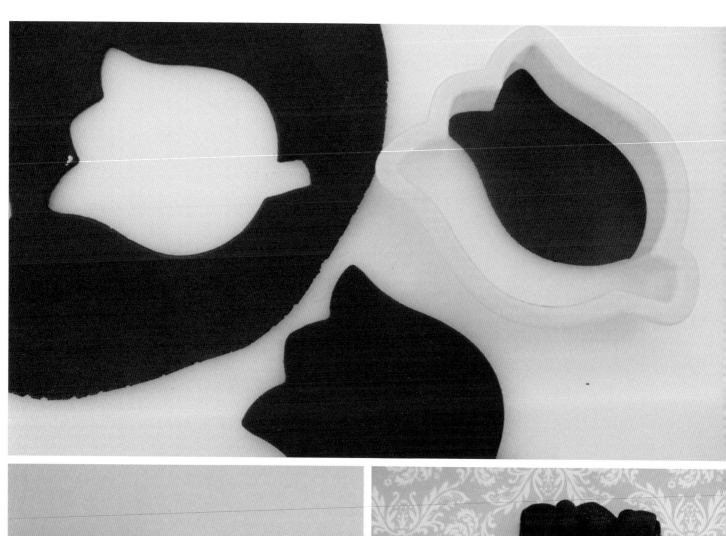

Tulips

These beautiful tulips make the perfect gift for Mum on Mother's day.
  Red is vibrant and always stands out however, these flowers can be made in the
color of your choice.

Instructions

1. Make the cookie dough of your choice cutting out tulip or any flower shapes, bake and leave to cool.
2. Color the fondant red and roll out to 1 mm (¾₄ in) thickness, using the same tulip cutter, cut out the base piece of icing.
3. Cut another piece using the same cutter but this time move the cutter to make two halves which resemble the top two petals overlapping.
4. Ruffle one side of each petal slightly to give the flower some character (a balling tool and petal pad can be used to create this effect). However, rubbing and bending the edges with two fingers will give a similar look. Stick the two half petals on top of the base piece of fondant using some piping gel or water.
5. Cut some green leaves from green colored fondant and stick at the base with piping gel.
6. Color some royal icing black and using a number 1 tip, pipe some stamens in the middle of the tulip.

Baby Blocks

Blocks can be used for a baby shower, christening or an infants birthday. They can be monogramed with letters or numbers or have simple cut outs such as the cute little feet, rocking horse and prams.

Instructions

1. Prepare cookies using the cookie mix of your choice, cut out squares with a square cutter and bake, leave to cool.
2. Roll out some fondant to 1 mm (³⁄₆₄ in) thickness and cut out squares. Using piping gel or sugar syrup dampen the cookie and place the fondant on top.
3. Roll out some more fondant in a contrasting color to 1 mm (³⁄₆₄ in) thickness and with a straight edged knife cut the border to 5 mm (¹³⁄₆₄ in) width and stick around the edges.
4. Using small cutters, details can be added to look like a babies building blocks. I have used a mold of a little pram for a simple and elegant cookie design.

Reindeers

Cookie cutters can sometimes be used to create designs in ways which they were not originally intended. The gingerbread man cutter when turned upside down, makes the ideal reindeer head.

Instructions

1. Prepare cookies using the cookie mix of your choice, cut out reindeer shapes with a gingerbread man cutter turned up side down (the legs become the antlers) bake and leave to cool.
2. Roll out some tan colored fondant to 1 mm ($\frac{3}{64}$ in) thickness. Using piping gel or sugar syrup dampen the head part of the cookie and place the fondant on top, trimming with a knife to leave off the antlers.
3. Roll some red fondant into a ball for the nose and do the same with the eyes using white and black colored fondant.
4. The antlers can be piped using some light brown royal icing in a piping bag with a number 2 tube.
5. Finish off with a liner brush dipped in black gel food coloring to add eyebrows and lashes.
6. Leave to dry for about 2 hours before storing or packaging.

Snowmen

These white snowmen are bright and festive, they stand out when placed amongst the traditional red and green which is so often used to decorate Christmas Cookies.

Instructions

1. Prepare cookies using the cookie mix of your choice, cut out snowmen with a cutter and bake, leave to cool.
2. Roll out some white fondant to 1 mm (3/64 in) thickness and using the cutter you used for the cookies cut out the fondant snowmen. Using piping gel or sugar syrup dampen the cookie and place the fondant on top.
3. Roll out some blue fondant for the hat using only the top part of the snowman cutter and trimming any excess fondant with a knife below the brim of the hat. Stick on top of the white fondant.
4. Using some orange colored fondant make a cone shape for a carrot nose then make some eyes using black fondant.
5. To make a scarf, color some fondant in red and green. Roll each color into long thin strips then twist the two colors together. Flatten with a rolling pin, and stick it to the neck area of the snowman. Some tassels can be added by cutting the end of the scarf using a small pair of scissors.
6. Use a liner brush to paint on the dots for a mouth and some stick like arms.
7. With royal icing stick three colored balls down the front of the snowman for the coat buttons.

Easter Eggs

Brightly colored egg shaped cookies will put a smile on anyone's face at Easter time. I have chosen to use geometric shapes to add color and detail to these simple yet effective Easter eggs. Pastel colors would also look great when creating these cookies.

Instructions

1. Prepare cookies using the cookie mix of your choice, cut out egg shapes with an oval cutter and bake, leave to cool.
2. Roll out some brightly colored fondant to 1 mm (³⁄₆₄ in) thickness and cut out ovals. Using piping gel or sugar syrup dampen the cookie and place the fondant on top.
3. Simple geometric cutters are great to give color to these simple cookies. Roll out fondant in various colors and cut out shapes to decorate as you wish. Simple circles always look good and add to the design.

Flowers

Flower shaped cookies make a beautiful floral bouquet and are great for any occasion.

Instructions

1. Make cookie dough of your choice cutting out flower shapes, bake and leave to cool.
2. Color the fondant to match your theme and roll out to 1 mm (³⁄₆₄ in) thickness, using the same flower cutter, cut out the base piece of icing.
3. Using piping gel or sugar syrup dampen the cookie and place the fondant on top.
4. The center for the flowers are made by rolling a ball of colored fondant and pressing into the mesh on a sieve, this forms tiny markings which resemble the flower center.

Cars, Trucks, Trains and Fire Engines

The perfect design for a little boy's birthday are these cars, trucks, trains and fire engines. They look especially exciting and colorful when arranged together in a bouquet or used singularly to match the theme of the occasion.

Instructions

1. Using your favorite recipe make cookies and cut into car, truck, train and fire engine shapes, bake and leave to cool.
2. Start by coloring the fondant with the desired food coloring then roll the fondant to a 1 mm (³⁄₆₄ in) thickness.
3. Cut out the shape using the same cutter which was used to cut out the cookie.
4. Using piping gel or sugar syrup dampen the cookie and place the fondant on top.
5. Have all the colors which are needed for the design pre-colored and ready at hand, then roll out and cut out the details.
6. For wheels use black colored fondant and cut circles, using a small balling tool push small dents to look like the nuts holding the wheels on.
7. Make windows from grey or black fondant and cut strips and squares to highlight a few details on the vehicles.
8. Use piping gel or syrup to stick on the embellishments.
9. Remember that every detail of a real vehicle doesn't have to be put on a tiny cookie, simple is best as the end product only needs to be an impression of what the real object looks like.

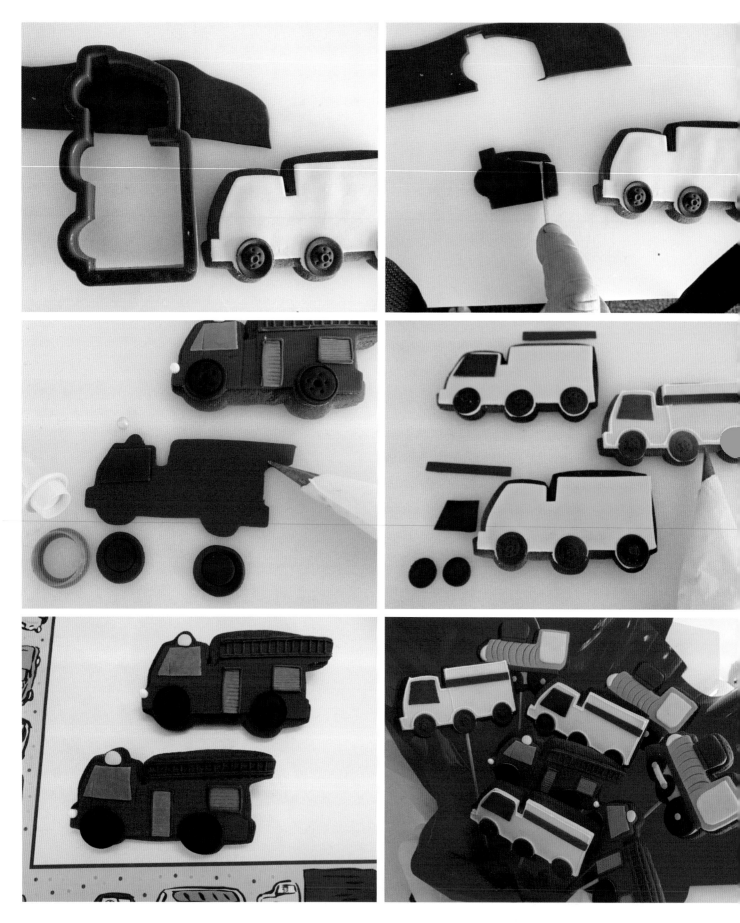

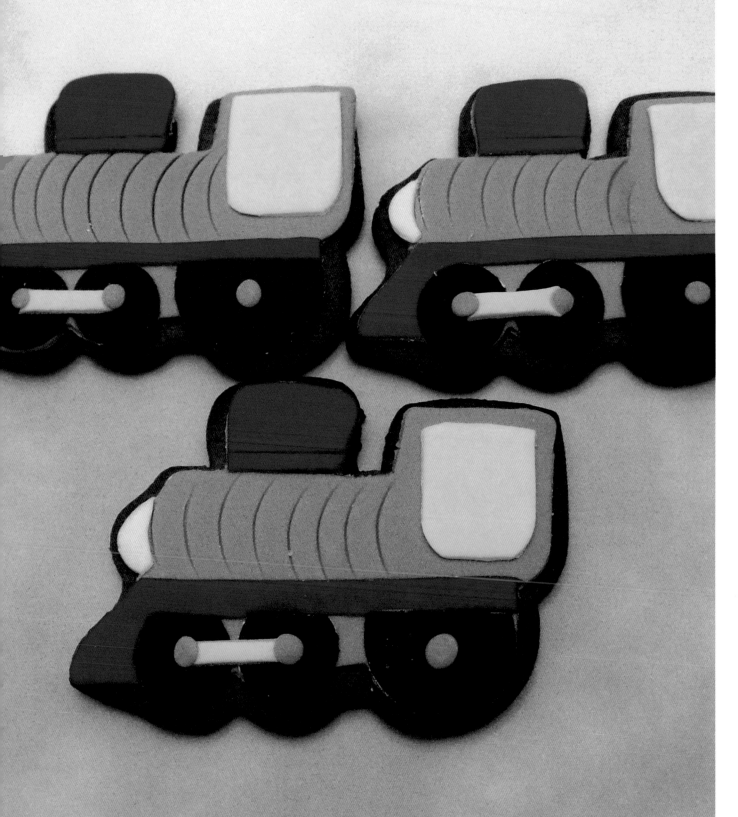

Chalk Board

A chalk board finish is another modern way to decorate special occasion cookies.
These could be used as a gift for a teacher or even for a wedding or special occasion, these unique cookies could be used as a place card for the table decoration.

Instructions

1. Color fondant black or use a ready made black fondant.
2. Roll out fondant to 1 mm (³⁄₆₄ in) thickness and cut out the desired shape to fit the cookie of your choice, I like to use a rectangle shape to represent a chalk board. Stick the fondant to the cookie using piping gel or sugar syrup.
3. Using some white food coloring or white petal dust, dilute with some rose spirit or white alcohol.
4. Take a large soft bristle paintbrush and gently smudge the black fondant to create a dusty looking surface. Now you're ready to embellish it in a creative way to suit the theme. To write on the board I use a liner brush that has been dipped in white gel paste food coloring.

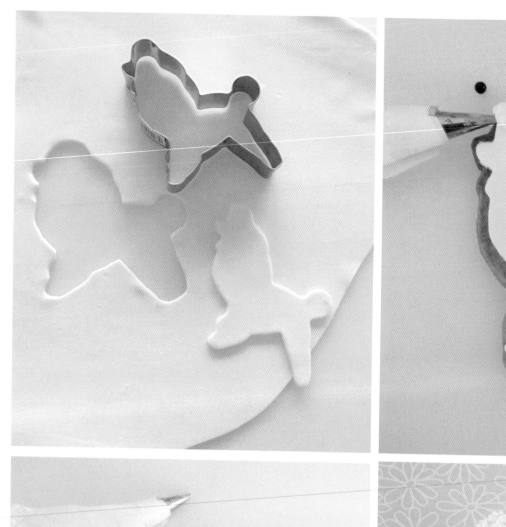

French Poodle

This white French Poodle is perfect for all dog lovers. It can be teamed with a handbag cookie, high heel shoe and Eiffel Tower cookie shapes for a French theme, perfect for a princess!

Instructions

1. Prepare cookies using the cookie mix of your choice, cut out the poodles with a cutter and bake, leave to cool.
2. Roll out some white fondant to 1 mm (¾₄ in) thickness and using the same poodle cutter that was used for the cookies cut out the fondant.
3. Use piping gel or sugar to dampen the top of the cookie, place the fondant on top and smooth.
4. Place some white royal icing in a piping bag with a number 2 tip and pipe where the fluffy parts of poodle would be, this can be as little or as much as you wish.
5. While the royal icing is still sticky dip the piped parts into a bowl of white hundreds and thousands, use a small ball of black icing for the eye.

Flood Work

Flood Work Instructions

Royal icing is used for flood work: to begin make the royal icing using the recipe on page 22.

Using a number 2 tube, pipe a border around the edge of the cookie which you are icing, do this on every cookie. Section off areas if there is more than one color per cookie.

Tip* If you use the same color for the border as the main body, the edge will be less visible however, a darker color can be used if the border needs to have a strong outline.

To make the icing runny for flooding inside the border, take some royal icing, place into a small bowl and mix with water, simply adding just a few drops at a time. Continue this until the icing is thick enough to flood without being too thin. It should go smooth when piped out onto the cookie yet be firm enough to stay within the piped border.

Add coloring if need be then fill a piping bag with the runny icing. A piping tip is not needed for running in as the tip can be simply cut with a pair of scissors

Details can be added while the icing is wet or it can be embellished after drying. To add details while the icing is still wet, it has to be done fairly quickly as the icing forms a crust on top within about 5 minutes. Speed is of the essence when doing work such as this.

Flood work takes a good 24 hours to dry out, it helps to have a dry, warm room temperature or even use an air flow heater to make the process quicker.

Tip* Mixing in the water can cause air bubbles, it is always good to cover the icing and let it "rest" for 30 minutes before piping. Once rested slowly stir being careful not to over beat, this will reduce the amount of air bubbles in the icing. Bubbles that appear on the surface of the cookie can be broken with a tooth pick while the flood work is still wet.

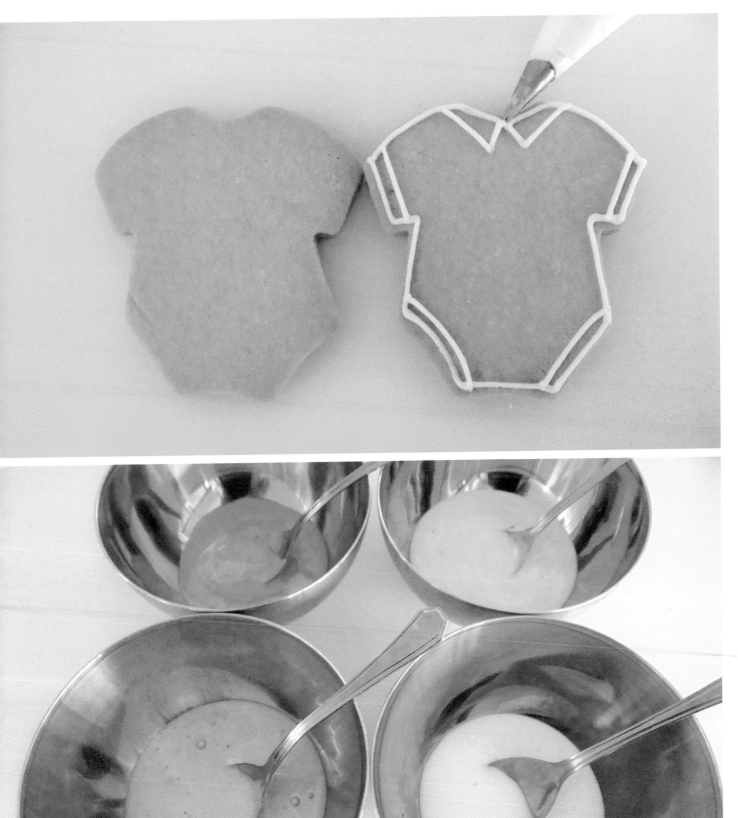

Easter Bunny

Chocolate at Easter time is usually in abundance so to receive an Easter treat which is not chocolate makes an alternative sweet gift.

Instructions

1. Make cookie dough of your choice cutting out the desired bunny shape, bake and leave to cool.
2. Color your icing and following the instructions for flood work (see page 58) cover your bunny cookies.
3. To add the white icing for the ears, have some white runny icing made up and ready to use. Simply pipe a short line on the pink before it sets.
4. To embellish the flood work bunny, place some white royal icing (see page 22) in a bag and pipe a white bunny tail. Before the royal icing forms a crust, sprinkle the tail with white nonpareils.
5. Pipe a tiny white eye and then with a liner brush paint a little black dot in the center for the pupil. With the liner brush still loaded in black food coloring paint in a mouth, eye lashes and eyebrow.

Baby Lettering and Number Cookies

These beautiful baby shower cookies were made using the flood work technique.

Creating the baby's name using the letter cutters would be another beautiful way to personalize a cookie bouquet.

Instructions

1. Make cookie dough of your choice cutting out the desired shapes, bake and leave to cool.
2. Using a number 2 icing tip, place some green royal icing into a piping bag to pipe the outline.
3. Follow the instructions for flood work as previously described (see page 58) filling inside the outline with the runnier icing. To add the spot design, have some white runny icing made up and ready to use. Simply pipe dots on the green before it sets.
4. Once the base color has been piped and set (drying time will take a few hours depending on weather conditions) the little flower embellishments can be added to the letter cookies.
5. Roll out a small piece of fondant and using a tiny blossom cutter, cut out flowers pushing in the center with a small balling tool, set aside to dry.
6. Once the flowers are set, stick them on the cookie with a tiny dab of royal icing.

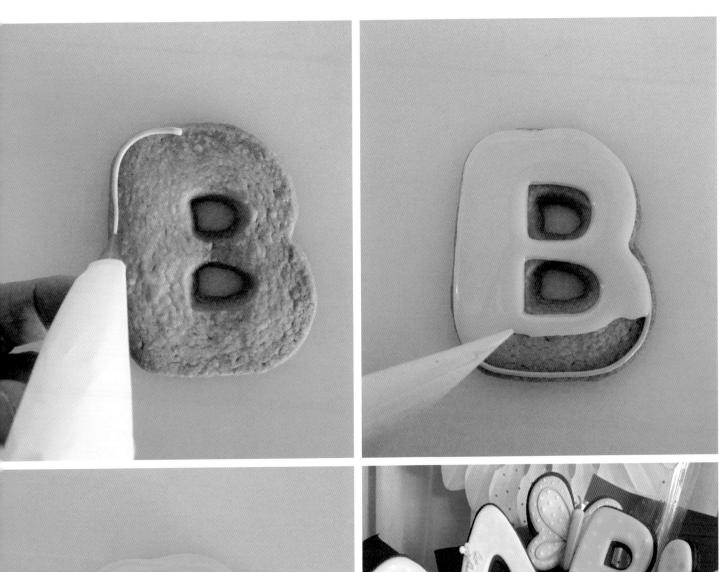

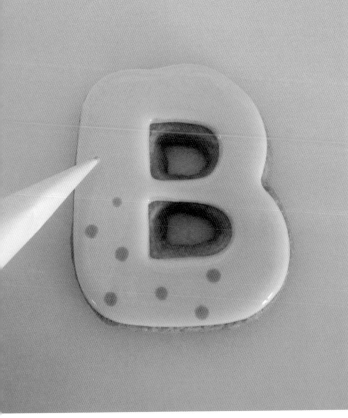

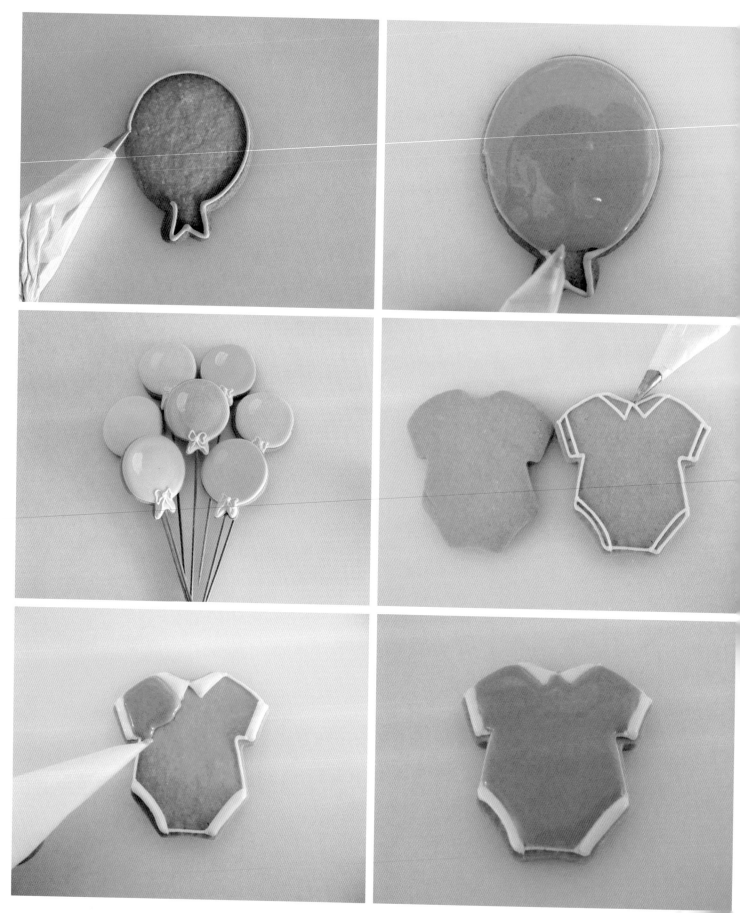

Balloons and Jump Suits

The soft pastel colors used to make balloons and jumpsuits are ideal when giving a gift to welcome the birth of a new baby. These would also look great in bright colors for any celebration.

Instructions

1. Make cookie dough of your choice cutting out balloon shapes and baby jumpsuits, bake and leave to cool.
2. Using a number 2 icing tip, place some white royal icing into a piping bag to pipe the outline before starting the flood work.
3. Make up some runny icing in pastels or bright colors, depending on your theme. Following the instructions for flood work (see page 58) fill inside the outline with the different colors and leave overnight to dry.
4. Embellish with piped lines for simple details.

Prams

Lime green is one of my favorite colors, teamed together with pink or blue. Prams can be used for baby showers, christenings or even a first birthday.

Instructions

1. Make cookie dough of your choice cutting out the pram shapes, bake and leave to cool.
2. Pipe a border around the edge of the cookie using a number 2 tip. Outline any areas where a different color would be used to keep them separate.
3. Flood royal icing using contrasting colors.
4. Finally finish off with piped details to define lines.
5. Add wheels using button molds to give a 3-D look to the pram.

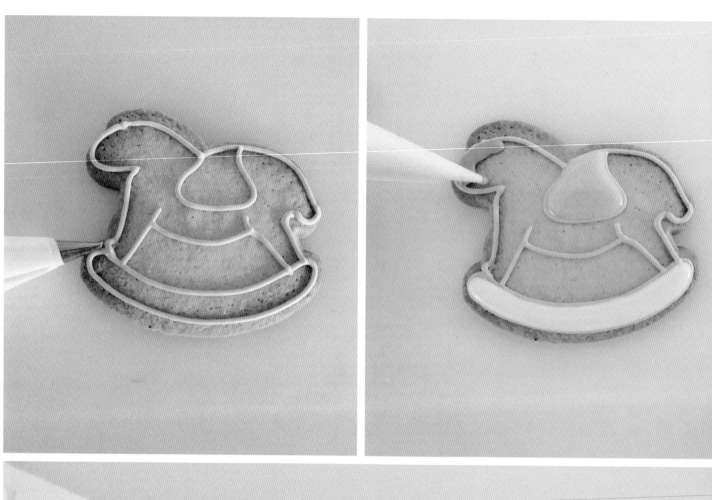

Rocking Horse

Rocking horses could be used for a carousel themed birthday party and are also a favorite for babies and infants functions such as christenings and baby showers.

Instructions

1. Make cookie dough of your choice cutting out the desired shapes, bake and leave to cool.
2. Pipe a border around the edge of the cookie using a number 2 tip. Outline any areas where a different color would be used to keep them separate.
3. Fill the body of the horse with pink runny icing, use a contrasting color for the saddle (I have used mauve), then add the curved base in another color. The floodwork should be left to dry until a crust forms on top and then proceed to add extra details.
4. Pipe some details such as reins, eyes, mouth and a swirly design on the rocker using royal icing and a number 1 tip (the icing should be a soft peak consistency to pipe the details).
5. For the mane and tail, fill a piping bag with yellow royal icing and pipe curved lines to resemble hair.

Candy Cane

Christmas candy canes add color to festive bouquets. Traditional red and green are my favorite colors to use however, cool blues and snow white colors would suit the theme as well.

Instructions

1. Make cookie dough of your choice cutting out the desired shapes, bake and leave to cool.
2. Pipe a border around the edge of the cookie using a number 2 tip. Outline any areas where a different color would be used to keep them separate.
3. Prepare your icing for flood work, red and green always go well for the festive season. Fill between the lines to give a twisted stripe effect.
4. Finally sprinkle on some edible glitter if you wish to give some sparkle to the candy canes.

Teapot

When holding a Kitchen Tea Party for a Bride to be, a commonly used theme is a teapot. These pretty green teapots with white spots and a hand piped rose are sure to be a favorite.

Instructions

1. Make cookie dough of your choice cutting out the desired shapes, bake and leave to cool.
2. Pipe a border around the edge of the cookie using a number 2 tip.
3. Using the flood work technique (see page 58) fill inside the outline with the runnier icing.
4. To add the spots, have some white runny icing made up and simply pipe dots on the green before it sets.
5. Once the base color has been piped and set (drying time will take a few hours depending on weather conditions) the embellishments can be added.
6. For the rose embellishments, fill a piping bag with white royal icing using a small petal tip. Take a toothpick and pipe tiny roses around the tip, only make a few petals as a large rose would look out of place. Once it has been piped lift the rose off the toothpick with some scissors and place on the teapot.

Wedding Dresses

When it comes to weddings there are so many pretty cookies that can be made. From a simple heart to go on the table as a 'bomboniere' or a pretty dress to reflect the bridal gown or just a simple flower to match the bridal bouquet.

The dresses here have been iced in flood work using royal icing however, they could be iced in fondant if you prefer.

Instructions

1. Using the desired cookie recipe, make dough and cut out dress shapes suitable for the occasion, bake and leave to cool.
2. Pipe a border around the edge of the cookie using a number 2 tip.
3. Using the flood work technique (see page 58) fill inside the outline with the runny icing.
4. Once the base color has been piped and set (drying time will take a few hours depending on weather conditions) the embellishments can be added.
5. The dresses can be embellished in many different ways. I decided to add various textures to the dress cookies. Fill a piping bag with some white royal icing using a number 2 tip. Pipe lines down the dress, or on the angle to resemble the flow of material.
6. The ruffles have been piped using a small rose petal tip number 59. Place the thicker side of the tube against the dress and wriggle the tip down the dress to make wavy lines.
7. Ruffles can also be piped across the dress to create a tiered effect.
8. The dress with pink roses has been painted using pink and white food coloring. Using a small paintbrush, mix pink coloring and white together to create a soft pink. Paint pink circles on the dress. Using a liner brush, paint white outlines to define the petals. The green leaves can be done using the same method, mixing green and white together then outline with a liner brush.
9. Small embellishments can be stuck on with royal icing in the form of tiny flowers or bows. Sanding sugar or edible glitter can also be sprinkled on the bodice to give a bit of sparkle.

HAND PIPING

Piping Instructions

Hand piping allows the freedom to personalize each cookie and make it your own. It is always helpful to draw a draft of the design on paper and have it near by to refer to.

I like to use gingerbread for this style of work as the contrast in color is much more effective, the gingerbread gives a lovely dark background which makes the piping stand out.

1. Prepare royal icing (see page 22) making sure it is not too stiff as it has to be piped out of a small icing tube.
2. Using a number 1 tube, fill the piping bag with royal icing. If using more than one color, prepare them all so they are ready to use.
3. Have the template with your sketched design beside the cookie so you can refer to it when necessary. A good tip is to start piping from the middle of the design to avoid working over the top of your work.
4. Once the design is piped, set cookies aside to dry, this will take a few hours depending on the weather and the thickness of the piping.

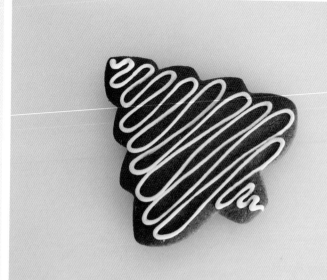

Christmas Cookies

Christmas is such a special time, to have a beautiful table setting with handmade Christmas gifts is very heart warming.

Gingerbread is a traditional Christmas specialty so begin by making the gingerbread dough and stamp out Christmas designs such as snowflakes trees, bells etc., bake and let them cool.

Instructions

1. Fill a piping bag with white royal icing using a number 1 tube in one bag and another using a number 2 tube.
2. Pipe patterns on top of the gingerbread. The snowflakes are simply lines piped from point to point with dots and smaller lines piped across.
3. This is the time where you can be creative, there are no rules when it comes to design so make it your own.

Inspired by Henna

Traditional henna designs are intricate and detailed. Piping with icing this way is something that takes a lot of practice. A number 0 or 1 tube is used to achieve this look.

Instructions

1. Make cookie dough of your choice cutting out the desired shapes, bake and leave to cool. (I have chosen a simple circular cutter for these as the detail is in the piping so the shape can remain simple).
2. Vibrant colors look fantastic for the designs so mix some brightly colored fondant and roll out to 1 mm (³⁄₆₄ in) thickness.
3. Cut out circles of the fondant and using piping gel or sugar syrup dampen the cookie and place the fondant on top.
4. Mix some dark brown food coloring into some soft peak royal icing.
5. Fill a piping bag with the brown royal icing using a number 1 or a number 0 piping tip depending on your piping experience.
6. Find a pattern that is not too detailed as piping takes time, have it beside your cookie and copy the pattern. It is not important to follow any pattern exactly as you see it just make it your impression and select parts that are not too tiny to pipe.

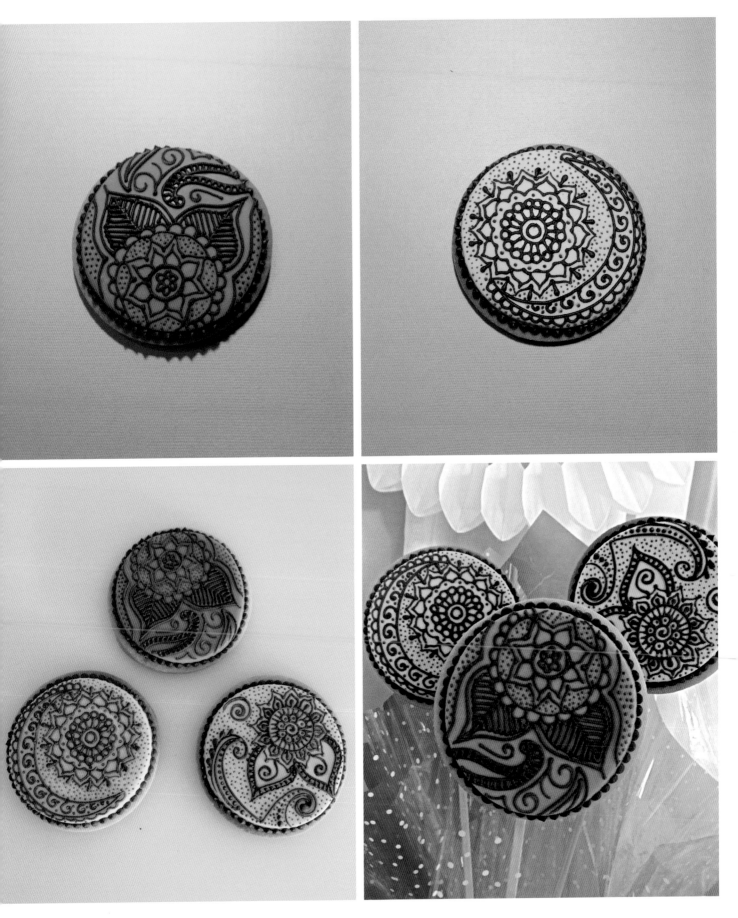

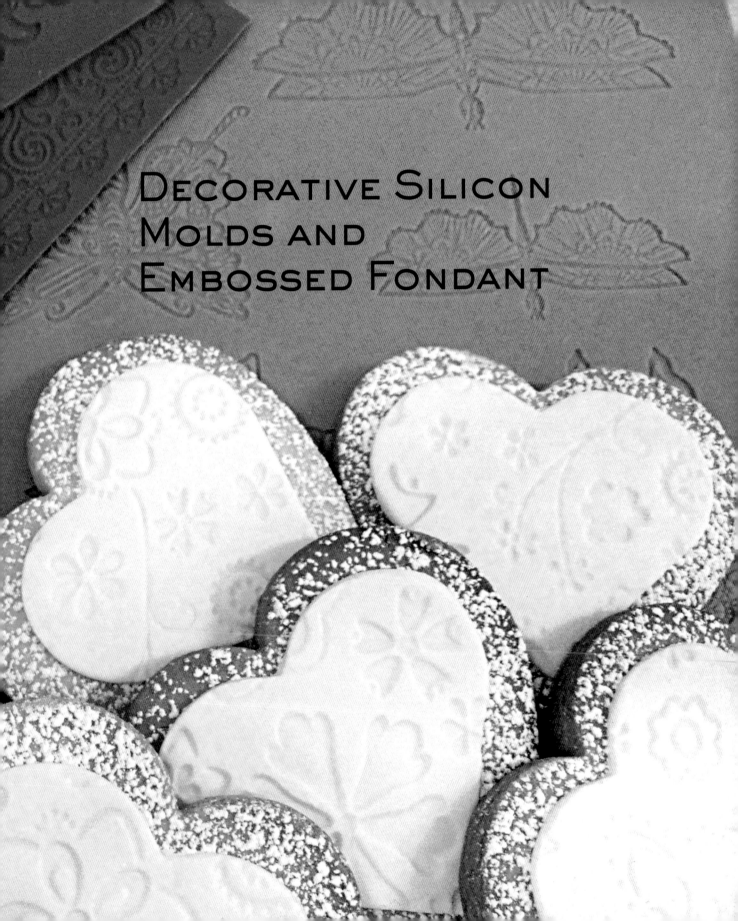

Decorative Silicon Molds and Embossed Fondant

Making Embellishments with Silicon Molds

There is so much choice when it comes to molds, there's a mold for almost everything so if there is a theme that a cookie needs to be designed around, molds just might be the way to go. I like to use a mold to further embellish a cookie whether it be iced initially with fondant or royal icing.

1. Take a piece of fondant in your hands and kneed it until it is soft and pliable. Tylose can be added to the fondant at this stage if a firm finish is what is needed.
2. With a thin dusting of cornstarch (cornflour) over the piece of fondant press it into the mold firmly, be sure to work it into the tiny grooves. Some molds are very intricate with tiny spaces where icing can get stuck. I like to use cornflour to dust the fondant, to prevent sticking, a thin smear of white fat brushed onto the fondant before pushing it into the mold is often successful as well.
3. When using a deep mold, it is often necessary to place it once filled with fondant into the freezer for a short time (5–10 minutes) so when it is removed the fondant doesn't squash and change shape.
4. Once it has been removed the design can be placed directly onto the iced cookie and stuck with a small dab of royal icing.

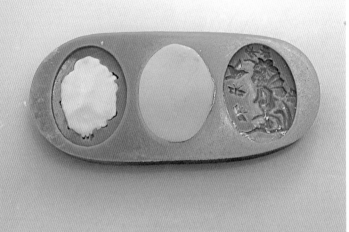

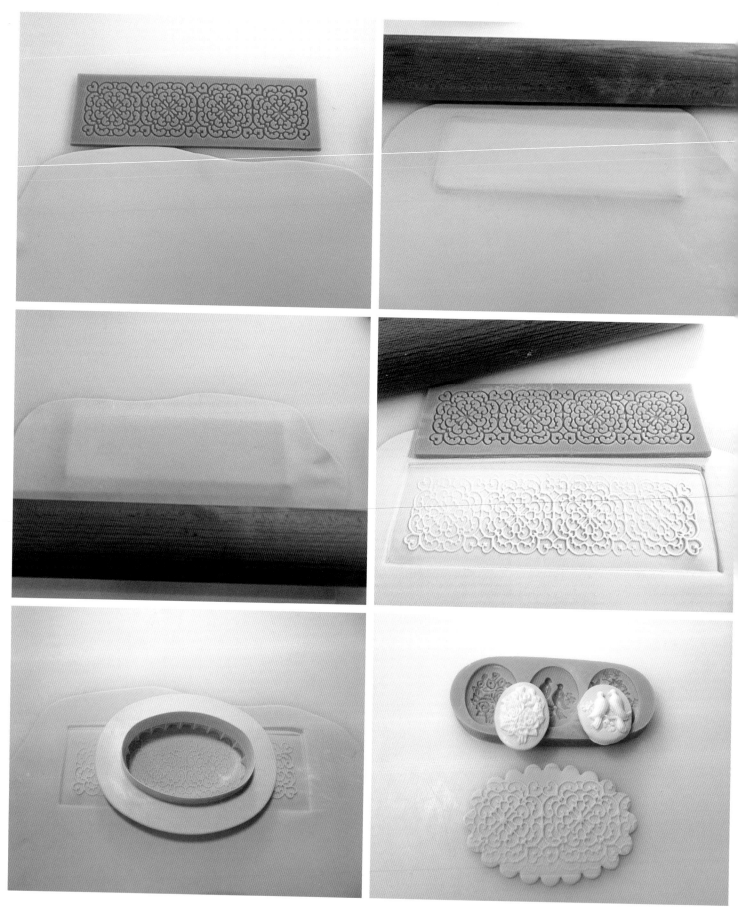

Embossed Fondant

Beautiful patterns using the embossing technique are easily accomplished. Embossing is a fast way of giving a professional finish in a few easy steps.

1. Roll fondant to 1 mm (³⁄₆₄ in) thickness and lightly dust with cornstarch (cornflour) to prevent sticking.
2. Take the embossing tool of your choice and simply press into the fondant, just hard enough to leave an impression.
3. Cut the embossed fondant into shapes using the same cutter which was used to cut out the cookie. Using piping gel or sugar syrup dampen the cookie and place the fondant on top.
4. Embellish with decorations suitable for the style of cookie being created.

Birds and Flowers

(Embossed fondant with birds and flowers using silicon molds)
These dainty cookie designs use two different techniques; embossing for the background and the use of molds to create a design to suit the theme. The vintage style embossing would also make a beautiful backdrop when using a cameo mold.

Instructions

1. Make cookie dough of your choice cutting out the desired shapes, bake and leave to cool.
2. Roll out some fondant to cover the cookie. The fondant should be rolled a little thicker than 1 mm (3/64 in) as it will go thinner when rolling over the embossing mold.
3. Place the embossing mold on the work surface and dust with a light covering of cornstarch (cornflour), place the rolled fondant over the top and with one motion push the rolling pin over to make an impression in the fondant. Using piping gel or sugar syrup dampen the cookie and stick the embossed fondant on top.
4. Using the bird and flower decorative silicon molds fill with contrasting colors (I have used white and blue) and pop out the design.
5. Place the molded fondant on to some previously cut white fondant with some piping gel to make it stick, then with more piping gel place this on the embossed surface on the cookie.
6. Pipe a border around the edge to finish off the design.

Handbags

What girl doesn't love a pretty handbag. This versatile cookie cutter is perfect for both young and old, the design options are endless, create a style of your own or use one of these pretty options.

Instructions

1. Prepare cookies as per baking instructions, use a handbag cookie cutter to make the basic shape, bake and leave to cool.
2. Color the fondant in contrasting colors, (I have used white, pink, black and beige). Roll fondant to a 1 mm (³⁄₆₄ in) thickness, using the same handbag cutter, stamp out the fondant and using piping gel or sugar syrup dampen the cookie and place the fondant on top.
3. Choose an embossing tool (there are many varieties) and press into the icing just firm enough to leave a pattern in the fondant.
4. Using the leftover fondant, hand mold some handles for the top of the handbag and finish off with silver or gold balls, you can stick these on with some piping gel.
5. Use your imagination to create other designs that compliment each other.

CAKE LACE

Cake Lace Instructions

One of the newest trends in decorating is cake lace. There are many brands of cake lace available, all of which are easy to use, be sure to follow the manufacturers instructions as the procedure varies depending on which brand you are using.

1. Once the cake lace is mixed, spread the mixture into a silicon lace mold, these can usually be placed in the oven on a very low heat to hasten the drying process. Always check the manufacturers notes for drying instructions and drying time.
2. When spreading the lace into the mold, take care to fill every tiny groove with the mixture.
3. Smooth the surface with a flat straight pallet knife so that there is no residue on top of the mold, a scraper could also be used.
4. When the lace is set, carefully peel it from the mold being careful not to break the lace, it is then ready to apply to either fondant iced cookies or cookies that have been flooded and dried.

Lace cookies

I have used lace on top of both fondant iced cookies and flood work iced cookies, either way is suitable for lace work to be placed over the top. These elegant lace molds are so pretty and delicate the uses are endless.

Instructions

1. Make cookie dough of your choice cutting out the desired shapes, bake and leave to cool.
2. Roll the fondant to 1 mm (³⁄₆₄ in) thickness.
3. Lightly dampen the top of the fondant and gently place and press the lace over it.
4. Take the cutter of your choice, which would be the same cutter used to cut out the cookie initially then cut the shape so the lace and the fondant cut together, this ensures that the lace covers the entire surface giving a neat and clean edge.
5. Using piping gel or sugar syrup dampen the cookie and place the fondant on top.
6. Finally be creative with your embellishments, add cachous, tiny cut out flowers, luster dusts or simply enhance the lace with some piping and leave to dry.

STENCILING

Stenciling Using an Airbrush

Stenciling using an air brush is a quick and easy way to achieve a smart crisp look. It can be done on fondant iced cookies or flooded cookies made with royal icing. I prefer to use fondant when stenciling as the surface is much smoother and there is less chance of the colors bleeding and smudging the outline.

Stencils come in many designs from simple geometric shapes to intricate pictures. Choose the design carefully remembering that simple designs often stand out better.

Always use cookies that bake fairly flat without bumps so the surface is smooth. Shortbread or gingerbread is best as it tends to bake evenly.

1. Once the cookies are baked leave to cool while preparing the icing.
2. Roll fondant to 1 mm (¾₄ in) thickness.
3. Place the stencil over the icing (it helps if you lightly brush the back of the stencil with a thin film of white vegetable shortening, this helps to keep the stencil in place). Give it a light roll with the rolling pin.
4. Fill the airbrush with the airbrush color of your choice, specialty cake suppliers will stock airbrush colorings.
5. Gently pull the trigger to fill the gaps with color. Don't over spray as this will cause the color to run under the stencil if it gets too wet.
6. Leave to dry for a few minutes and then carefully peel back the stencil, working from one side to the other and leave to dry thoroughly, avoid dragging the stencil across the icing as this will smudge the artwork.
7. Cut out fondant shape using the same cookie cutter as originally used for the cookie, then dampen the cookie surface with sugar syrup or piping gel and place the fondant on top.
8. For an extra touch of decoration, you can create monogramed cookies using letter cutters, initials can be added at this stage to personalize the cookie or simply cut out hearts, birds or figures of your choice.

Stenciling Using Royal Icing

There are many beautiful stencil designs available in cake decorating and craft stores. Stenciling gives the finished product a formal elegant look as the design is uniform with clean lines.

1. Roll out your fondant to 2 mm (5/64 in) thickness.
2. Choose the desired stencil to decorate your cookies and place on top of the fondant.
3. Prepare the royal icing (see page 22) it should be soft enough to be easily spread over the stencil. If it is too runny the icing is susceptible to going under the stencil resulting in smudged, undefined lines.
4. Spread the royal icing with a pallet knife or scraper over the stencil, not too thick and with one or two forward strokes.
5. Peel the stencil back carefully from the fondant. The royal icing will crust quickly, once it has crusted slightly a cutter can be used to stamp out the shape.
6. Brush the top of the cookie with sugar syrup or piping gel, and place the cut out fondant on top of the cookie and leave to dry.

PRINTED IMAGES

Applying Printed Images

When making a personalized cookie for an individual person or company, a printed edible image is a good option as a logo or photo on top can look stunning. Printing onto edible paper enables the user to produce professional artwork or photos onto a small disc to place on top of the cookie, this keeps them all uniform.

While the initial outlay is a little expensive, using prints this way saves time in the long run which is well worth the investment when making a lot of cookies.

1. First make a draught of the image that you need printed, being sure to check that the size of each picture fits onto the cookie. If you have your own printing device which has food coloring cartridges, not ink as it is not edible, it is just a matter of loading in the blank edible paper, hit print and presto! Ready in a flash! Cake decorating stores often have the equipment to print for you if you don't have a printer of your own.
2. Next, cut out the picture with a pair of scissors.
3. Prepare fondant the same as you would for icing any cookies, roll out a 1 mm (³⁄₆₄ in) thickness.
4. Dampen the top of the icing with a thin smear of water, just enough to make the icing tacky not too wet.
5. Peel the plastic backing from the image and press onto the fondant to make it stick.
6. Use a cookie cutter to stamp out around the print which can then be placed on top of the cookie using piping gel or sugar syrup to make it stick.
7. Embellishments can be piped around the edge of the disk or it can be left plain.

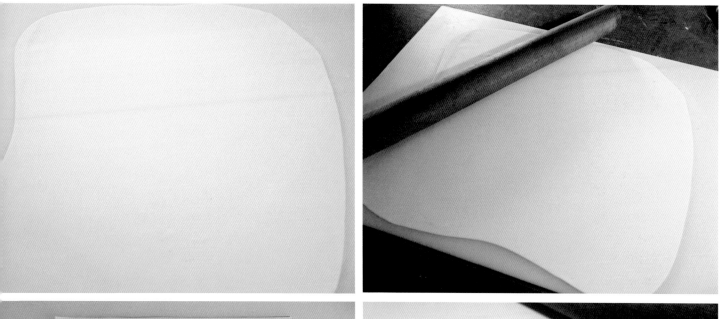

Logo Cookies

Cookies are a great form of advertising when using a company logo or emblem on top. They can be used as a promotional tool or can be given out as a way of saying thank you at an event. To personalize your cookie with a unique design is very special, anyone receiving a cookie such as these are sure to be delighted.

Instructions

1. Roll fondant to 1 mm (³⁄₆₄ in) thickness.
2. Lightly dampen the top of the fondant and gently place and press the cut out logo on top. Take a round cutter, which would be the same size or just a little larger than the edible image and cut the fondant with the printed logo on top.
3. Place on top of a dampened cookie using piping gel or sugar syrup.
4. If there is space a border can be piped around the edge or just leave plain.

BOUQUETS

Making a Cookie Bouquet

When you receive a handmade gift it is guaranteed to put a smile on your face. Gifts such as these are very special as they are so visually appealing, they always create interest and are a great talking point. They look stunning on a dessert table or as a center piece for a dinner party. When creating a bouquet for a children's party they can be handed out to each child to take home in place of the traditional party bags. The cookies themselves don't need to be difficult, it is often the simplest of designs which attract the most attention. Here are some simple steps to help create the perfect bouquet for your embellished cookies.

Presentation
Presentation is what finishes off the end product. To make your master pieces even more appealing it is very important to color co-ordinate the packaging and include embellishments to reflect the theme. If care is taken to make your beautiful treats look good it will often give the opinion that they will also taste good!

Packaging
Cookies need to be sealed in order to keep them from spoiling. Packaging individual cookies is a must, as cookies absorb moisture from the air and go soft and stale quickly if they are not protected. Once your cookies have been decorated make sure that the icing and any embellishments are completely dry before sealing in a bag.

Poly propylene bags or cellophane bags are a great way to protect your cookies. When making large amounts a heat sealer would be a quicker way to package, when packaging only a few cookies the bags can be tied off with a ribbon which looks great as well.

Ribbons, Paper and Labels
Simple ribbons and labels make the project complete.

A gift tag or card tied around the base gives a personal touch, especially if the bouquet is being given as a gift. Equally a lovely bow tied around a box or tin will make it special and add color. I like to use the glossy floristry paper to line the boxes and ceramic containers as it doesn't crush too easily and looks clean and fresh.

Display Containers

Glass or plastic containers are a great option for keeping your cookies looking and tasting great. When making a bouquet, a ceramic pot or small timber crate are good bases, cardboard boxes such as floristry boxes are also great and colorful too. Be sure to not put too many cookies in as the boxes are not heavy enough to support the cookies which are top heavy when place on skewers.

Making the Box

1. Purchase a length of timber from the hardware store, I have used pine which is 90 mm (3½ in) wide and 600 mm (24 in) long. The thickness is 19 mm (¾ in).
2. Cut the timber into 130 mm (5¼ in) lengths as shown.
3. Assemble the pieces of timber so that they form a square, using 25 mm (1 in) nails hammer the pieces together to secure. Two or three nails at each end will be sufficient.
4. To create the base of the box, nail a square piece of thick cardboard or a Masonite cake board to the bottom (140 mm (5½ in) square).
5. Paint the box in the color of your choice using a can of spray paint, leave to dry outside.
6. Brightly colored floristry paper or tissue paper can be used to decorate the box. Push some floristry foam into the box to hold the paper in place and then you are ready to insert the cookies into the foam to create a beautiful display. Ribbon can also be tied around the box to make the perfect gift.

About the Author

Robyn King is a qualified pastry chef with 40 years' experience in the industry. She is a very experienced cake/cookie decorator/teacher of the craft and regularly does demonstrations at specific functions. Robyn belongs to cake/cookie decorating groups where she is able to not only share many years of knowledge but also learn new techniques and tips from other members.

In 2013 Robyn opened her own shop *The Embellished Cake Creations* supplying decorating equipment, baking products, and running classes – whilst continuing to keep her hand in decorating wedding/special occasion cakes and cookies.

Embellished Cookies is Robyn's first book.